D0121096

the
denbook

jo schofield • fiona danks

F

FRANCES
LINCOLN

For Connie, Dan, Edward,
Hannah and Jake

Frances Lincoln Ltd

www.goingwild.net

The Den Book
Copyright © Frances Lincoln 2016
Text copyright © Jo Schofield and Fiona Danks 2016
Photographs copyright © Jo Schofield and Fiona
Danks 2016

First Frances Lincoln edition: 2016

Jo Schofield and Fiona Danks have asserted
their right to be identified as the authors of this
work in accordance with the Copyright, Designs
and Patents Act 1988 (UK).

All rights reserved. No part of this publication
may be reproduced, stored in a retrieval system
or transmitted in any form, or by any means,
electronic, mechanical, photocopying, recording
or otherwise, without either prior permission in
writing from the publisher or a licence permit-
ting restricted copying, in the United Kingdom.
Such licences are issued by the Copyright Licensing
Agency, Saffron House, 6-10 Kirby Street, London
EC1N 8TS.

A catalogue record for this book is available
from the British Library.

ISBN 978-0-7112-3766-7

Printed and bound in China

9 8 7 6 5 4 3 2 1

This book contains some potentially dangerous
activities. Please note that any reader or anyone
in their charge taking part in any of the activities
described does so at their own risk. Neither the
authors nor the publisher can accept any legal
responsibility for any harm, injury, damage, loss or
prosecution resulting from the use or misuse of the
activities, techniques, tools and advice in the book.
   It is illegal to carry out any of these activities
on private land without the owner's permission,
and you should obey all laws relating to the
protection of land, property, plants and animals.

Quarto is the authority on a wide range of topics.

Quarto educates, entertains and enriches the lives of
our readers – enthusiasts and lovers of hands-on living.

www.QuartoKnows.com

CONTENTS

INTRODUCTION

Are you a den dreamer, a den designer and a den builder? If so, this book is for you. *The Den Book* is all about escaping outdoors to use your imagination, to be creative, to make up the rules, to explore the wild world and to create magical hideaways in which to spend your time.

An indoor den created in an upturned sofa or a cosy base camp assembled under a table are great, but these borrowed spaces always have to be tidied up after use. Outdoor dens, though, can be built anywhere, from anything, and in any weather. They are spaces in which you are designer, problem-solver, builder and owner all in one. Your den may be messy; it may be a bit ramshackle, but that doesn't matter – it will be yours – a place for hiding, sharing adventures, making up stories, facing challenges, scheming and planning. It may be hidden from the grownups and will be built to your scale.

An outdoor den might be a hideaway in a garden hedge, a stick fort in the woods, a leafy shelter for spying on wildlife, or a little house nestling among the branches of a favourite tree. It may be a driftwood shelter at the beach, an old shed converted into a mud cafe, a green leafy hidey-hole in a living willow dome or a Hobbit hole among ancient tree roots. Dens may lead you into other worlds or times, providing a portal into a parallel world where woodland warriors, forest fairies or dangerous dragons hide among the trees. Or perhaps your den is on a miniature scale, a castle for toy soldiers, an igloo for a teddy bear or an ice palace for a fierce, frosty fairy.

Natural dens made in public spaces are there for the taking; destruction is part of the process, so don't be disappointed if your precious hideaway becomes the starting point for someone else's den. Learn from how others build their dens; be creative and share ideas. We hope *The Den Book* will inspire you and your friends to get outdoors, feel at home in wild places and enjoy all sorts of incredible den-building adventures.

WOODLAND DENS

WONDERFUL WOODLAND HIDEAWAYS

We think that woodlands are the best places in which to make outdoor dens, especially those made among twisted roots, in ancient hollow trees and from loose sticks and leaves gathered from the ground.

These pages are packed with ideas for woody hideaways: discover places to play and to hide; places where you can share forest feasts and listen to stories and places where you can watch wildlife and disappear into imaginary worlds. Some of these woodland hideaways may be good enough to stay for the whole night – if you are brave enough!

WOODLAND DEN TIPS

LEAN STICKS AGAINST A FIRM STRUCTURE

• The best materials for woodland dens are fallen branches, sticks and piles of dry, dead leaves. Only use sticks that are firm; avoid any that are soft or rotten.

• Take along a tarp or some plastic sheeting to enhance natural den materials.

• Den locations: over a ditch, inside a hollow tree, leaning against a fallen tree trunk, or among exposed roots. Or, how about a den in a tree, perhaps on a small platform, among low branches or between the trunks of a multi-stemmed tree?

• Many woodland dens are built from long sticks placed on a forked branch to make a shelter. If you can't find a suitable tree for this, see page 20 for tepee-building tips.

ROOF LATTICE BUILT OVER DRY DITCH

TARP ROOF AND WALLS

LEAN LARGE STICKS AGAINST A TREE

TEST GROUND FOR COMFORT

LEAN-TO DEN

This was our favourite den ever; we returned to it over and over again for magical family picnics and adventures, even on rainy days. Creating a good den like this is a wonderful family project to work on together.

HOW TO MAKE OUR FAVOURITE WOODLAND DEN

● Find a large fallen tree beside an open area. Collect three long branches from the woodland floor, then bind them together to make a frame against the fallen tree. You can use natural binding such as blackberry runners, honeysuckle, ivy or wild clematis stems, or take along some string.

● Now add more branches over the original frame, tying each one in place. Finally, weave twigs and stems through the framework to make a lattice.

This den is thatched with grasses, but dead leaves would also work well as a roof. Starting at ground level, lay grasses or leaves over the lattice, working all the way up to the top until you have a thick covering. You may wish to sweep the floor to make a smooth place to sit, or make a bed of leaf-litter to lie on.

DENS FOR WARRIORS AND OUTLAWS

Deep in the wild woods, warriors and outlaws may be looking for a place to set up camp. They could need a base where they can lie low and spy on the enemy, or maybe they need a fort to defend themselves from fierce invaders? The best warrior dens should be hidden, perhaps in a random pile of sticks, camouflaged with greenery or among bushes.

WARRIOR DEN ARMOURY

Wild woodland warriors should do their best to blend in with the surroundings with camouflaged clothing, green rubber boots, and war paint made from mud, clay or ground-up chalk.

All warrior dens need a stock of wild wood-weapons (see below and pages 18–19) and a target on which to practise using them. Take a look at some of our suggestions for making and using various pieces of armoury. You may also like to take along head torches and walkie-talkies to keep in touch with each other when you are out and about.

BENDY HAZEL BOW

Bow and arrow Make simple bows from sticks of bendy wood such as freshly cut hazel. Cut a little notch near each end of the stick. Tie a length of string firmly around one notch, and then pull the string tight enough to make the stick curve, before tying the string tightly around the other notch. Collect a few straight sticks to use as arrows.

WARRIOR DEN ARMOURY

Sword Great little swords can be made from two straight sticks. Bind a short stick tightly onto a longer stick with plenty of string. Or find a slightly bendy stick, bend one end round and tie it in place to make a more authentic handle (see right).

Spear Choose a very straight stick and whittle one end to a point with a sharp knife. Or you could try making a metal tip by flattening the head of an old spoon. Insert this into a split on the end of a spear, binding it tightly in place with string.

Plastic blow pipe Use a narrow plastic pipe as a blow pipe. Make kebab-skewer darts with a cone on one end: cut out a small semi-circle of thin card, fold it into a cone and tape onto a skewer. Check the cone is exactly the right size to fit snugly down the pipe. Blow the darts at a target such as an egg box.

Shield Use old saucepan lids or make shields from green willow. Bend the willow into a shield shape and attach one or two sticks across it with raffia. Weave grasses or reeds through it to secure.

Safety tip Take care when using knives or sticks – never use weapons on people.

SWORD WITH BENT-STICK HANDLE

SPEAR MADE WITH FLATTENED SPOON

PUSH SPOON HANDLE INTO SPEAR END

SWORD AND WOVEN SHIELD

SPEAR COLLECTION

BLOWPIPE DART IN TARGET

PLASTIC BLOW-PIPE

LINE UP THE STICKS TIE TOGETHER AT ONE END

ARRANGE STICKS EVENLY IN A TEPEE SHAPE

WEAVE WITH LEAVES

WOODLAND TEPEE

This freestanding natural tepee in a woodland glade is a perfect place to share a picnic with friends or make a warm drink.

HOW TO MAKE A WOODLAND TEPEE

● Look for five 2m/6ft long sticks, or ask an adult to cut some from a living hazel tree. Lay the sticks on the ground in a neat heap; tie them tightly together near one end.

● Stand the sticks up, tied ends at the top. Pull the bottom of each stick outwards to form an evenly-spaced tepee shape. If the sticks are fairly upright, your tepee will shed rain better. Push the end of each stick into the ground.

● Weave leaves, twigs and small branches between the sticks to make a lattice (see page 15). For a waterproof tepee, cover the sticks with a tarp. Furnish your tepee as you wish.

KELLY KETTLE TIPS

The perfect way to enjoy a safe outdoor fire and heat up water for soup or a hot drink. Fill the outside chamber of the Kelly kettle with water at home. In an open area of ground, build a small fire of very dry twigs in the metal pan. Light the fire and carefully place the metal chimney over the pan to heat up the water. Consult the Fire Safety Guidelines on page 140 before you start.

RIVER FISHING DEN

What better way to enjoy a magical spot beside a river than to make a den and stay a while? It might be the perfect place to watch riverside wildlife, to try a spot of fishing, or to have a picnic. This den was made with long sticks supported by the fork of a tree and later thatched with loose bits of vegetation washed up by the river.

Watching river wildlife Look out for dragonflies, mayflies and other insects flying over the water or feeding on waterside plants, as well as for fish rising to the surface to catch insects and for birds swooping down to feed.
Crayfishing In some rivers there is a problem because of too many introduced signal crayfish. They are recognizable by their bright red claws and can be

easily caught. All you need is a plastic mushroom box, some string and some bacon. Attach string to each corner of the box and then fix some bacon on its base. Lower the trap into the water and wait; if you are lucky, you will attract several crayfish. Cook them in boiling water for a tasty riverside snack.

DIY fishing Make a simple fishing rod from a long, straight stick with string tied to one end. Tie a small hook onto the end of the string, then bait with a flour-and-water paste. This simple rod may not catch you a fish, but it is fun to try while enjoying being beside a river. Also try fishing with a simple hand-line.
Safety tips Always make sure you are with an adult when partaking in any waterside activities. Handle crayfish with caution; they have very powerful claws. Remember, too, that fishing hooks are very sharp, so take special care when casting your rod.

STICK FISHING ROD

CRAYFISH TRAP

GARDEN DENS & TREEHOUSES

GARDEN GETAWAYS

It's not always easy to get to the woods and you may be worried about where to go, or being told off for damaging plants or disturbing wildlife. So how about making space for wild getaways and playspaces in the garden at home or at a friend's or relative's house?

Take over a wild corner Perhaps whoever looks after the garden will be happy for you to take over a wild corner behind some bushes, against a fence or in a secret place in a hedge? Or maybe an adult could put up some trellis and plant a few bushes to screen off a small area from the rest of the garden? This should become YOUR space, where you can make a mess and create your own little world for creating dens, playing, making mud pies and hiding away.

Adopt a shed Maybe there is a shed at the bottom of the garden just waiting for you to adopt it? Decorate it, inside and out, with natural and collected materials, transforming it into a place in which you can play shops and cafes, create a mini-museum (see page 119) or turn it into a sleep-out den with a couple of sleeping platforms.

MUD KITCHEN

MUD CAFE

An old shed makes a wonderful mud cafe for entertaining your friends. You need a good place nearby to collect mud (not the best flowerbeds!). Furnish the mud cafe with a box cooker and wood, then equip it with old pots and pans, ladles, teapots, cake trays and plastic pots. Now you will be all set to serve.

PLAY-EQUIPMENT DENS

Take a new look at the play equipment in your garden; perhaps you don't play with it very often. Try transforming a swing, climbing frame or goal into something much more fun and magical.

Alien spaceship It didn't take long to turn this trampoline into an amazing alien spaceship. A roll of corrugated cardboard and some old rugs were wrapped around the trampoline's base, then fixed in place with pegs to create a secret cabin. A few spyholes were cut in the corrugated cardboard, and a specially defended trap door was made out of a bodyboard. Cardboard rings

ALIEN SPACESHIP DETAILS

TINFOIL PORTHOLES

CONTROL CENTRE

Alien slime recipe

Add a few drops of green food colouring to some water in a bowl. Slowly mix together with cornflour until it reaches the consistency of slime. The best alien slime goes hard when you squeeze it, but turns into a gloopy liquid when you release the pressure and let it run through your fingers... have fun!

Quality rocket-fuel potion

Our rocket needed a fuel with the following ingredients: a human hair, a twig, a handful of cut grass, a cup of squidgy mud, three drops of purple food colouring, a pinch of pixie dust (see page 34), a speck of gold and a square of chocolate. Mix well. What recipe does your own rocket run on?

wrapped in tinfoil became portholes, the control centre was a decorated cardboard box, and the lookout tower was under an umbrella at the top. When the spaceship was completed and ready for lift-off, the astronauts used high-quality rocket fuel and energetic bouncing to blast it off into space in search of alien-friendly planets. To make the space experience more authentic, have a go at making thixotropic alien slime and a rocket-fuel potion.

UMBRELLA DEN

It's pouring with rain outside, but don't let that stop you making a great outdoor den. Gather up as many umbrellas as you can and build a colourful den in the garden or at the park, or perhaps out in the woods?

Umbrella-den tips If making the den in your garden, arrange outdoor chairs in a circle, with the seats facing outwards. For umbrella dens in the park, you could perhaps use a park bench or some play equipment as a starting point?
   Place the umbrellas over the chairs so they overlap each other and the handles don't poke into the den. In this den, only the handle of the clear umbrella at the top sticks into the middle. Secure the umbrellas in place with pegs and cord, especially if it's a windy day. Cover the ground with a tarp or waterproof rug. Add some little seats and enjoy a rainy-day picnic.

TIE-ON GUY ROPES

STICK TENT PEG

PEG FABRIC ON LINE

WASHING-LINE DEN

A long washing line is a perfect starting point for making a tent-style den.

Throw a large piece of fabric such as an old sheet, blanket, curtain or sari over the washing line. Make more space by pinching the fabric together and tying some string around it (above left). Pull the string outwards to make a guy rope, then tie it round a stick or tent peg stuck into the ground. Make an entrance from two sticks of bendy willow or hazel. Push the sticks into the ground at one end of the tent, tie them onto the washing line to make an arch, then peg the fabric onto the arch (opposite).

FAIRY TENT

This beautiful tent made with brightly coloured saris is dressed fit for a fairy princess. She can sit at her dressing table in front of her flower-draped mirror and apply her pixie dust make-up. Little bottles of petal perfume and flower lotions line her shelves, and soft toys are arranged on bean bags. What a perfect place to laze around on dreamy feather pillows, dress for the ball, make spells or share a fairy feast of afternoon tea and scones with jam.

When night comes the fairy den is transformed into a magical glowing bower

with strings of lights and night-light lanterns (see pages 82–83). The fairies put on a shadow puppet show, bewitching the invited audience with long menacing shadows which dance and leap across the pink tent walls. (The fairies had made cardboard cut-out puppets and shone torches behind them.)

Flower chains These can be made with all sorts of flowers as well as daisies. Gently split a flower stem with your nail to make a small hole. Thread the stem of another flower through the hole. Repeat over and over again to make a beautiful chain.

Pixie dust Mix three drops of food colouring, two teaspoons of salt, a few

FAIRY TENT DETAILS

FLOWER CHAINS

PIXIE DUST ON PETAL PERFUME

tiny petals or blossoms and whatever other magical-looking or fairy-like ingredients you can find outdoors.

Petal perfume and lotions Collect a few petals from sweet-smelling flowers (try to collect fallen petals) and add to water with a few drops of food colouring. Or gently crush rose or lavender petals using a pestle and mortar, add a little water and squeeze through muslin. If you wish, you can add the perfumed liquid to a basic, odourless hand and body lotion.

Fairy picnic Set out a tiny picnic on a mossy tablecloth, perhaps with flower decorations, walnut-shell bowls, petal plates and a miniature feast.

FLOWER DECORATIONS

FAIRY PICNIC

GARDEN-TABLE DEN

Grownups rarely venture into under-table land, so it's a great place for games and adventures. A table is also a good starting point for a den; it's on your scale and it will have a good strong roof. Garden tables tend to be less precious than indoor tables and, of course, there's no danger of damaging the carpet.

Perhaps you could make your table den on a theme; maybe it's a cowboys' and cowgirls' campout high in the mountains of the Wild West, or a soldier's secret hideout tucked away deep behind enemy lines. Choose a good spot to make

the den, slightly out of the way but with room to fight off the enemy. Turn chairs round the wrong way and lean them against the table to make walls. Cover the table and chairs with green and brown fabrics such as old curtains or tablecloths, garden netting or some camouflage material.

Add twigs and leaves cut from garden shrubs to provide a better disguise. Make an entrance; this one was made by leaning two folded chairs together to make a doorway shaped like an upside-down V. You might decorate the entrance with natural treasures brought back from a walk or borrowed from your Collector's Museum Den (see page 119). Add a flagpole; many garden tables have a hole in the middle for an umbrella – and handy for a broomstick flagpole. Make a natural flag from a rhubarb leaf with a scary face cut out of it.

COWBOY CAMPOUT IDEAS

BROOM FLAG POLE

ANTLER AND FEATHERS

Home-made weapons This campout was armed with an array of simple weapons, many of them carved from sticks collected from the woods. Perhaps you could use a special pen knife (see Tool and Weapon Safety Guidelines on page 140) to carve a rifle, a samurai sword or a dagger. Alternatively, make a simple sword from a couple of sticks (see page 18) or simply gather together a good stick collection and apply a good dose of imagination...

STICK 'WEAPONS'

COVER WITH FABRIC

PEG FABRIC AROUND
THE ENTRANCE

GARDEN TEPEE

These garden tepees may look rather professional, but they were put together very quickly, from a few garden canes and some old sheets and pieces of fabric.

HOW TO MAKE A GARDEN TEPEE

● You will need five or six garden canes about 2m-2.5m/6-8ft long. Hold them together in a bundle. Wrap a rubber band tightly round the canes about 30-60cm/1-2ft from the end.

● Stand the canes upright in your chosen spot, with the rubber band at the top. Pull the canes apart at the bottom, leaving a larger gap between two of the canes as an entrance. When the spacing is right, push the end of each cane into the ground to fix them in place.

● Fix the fabric to the cane frame with pegs or clips and make sure it fits snugly. Decorate with a dream-catcher or some flowers and leaves and place a box or log inside as a seat.

● For an entrance, secure fabric back from the doorway with pegs facing away from the opening. Or make an arch from bendy wood.

● A tepee made with dark-coloured fabric may need a window, so use twisted creeper or bendy wood woven into a ring and pegged in place on the frame to allow light in and enable you to keep a look out for visitors.

TREEHOUSES

A good treehouse is perhaps the ultimate den. It's the perfect place to hide away in a leafy hideout, offering an owl's-eye view on the world below.

A treehouse can be anything from a basic platform to a simple shack cobbled together from a few old planks and plywood offcuts, to a more elaborate, little house built up among the branches. The first thing to think about when making a treehouse is safety; you must choose a large, healthy tree with no dead wood, and then you need to make sure that the treehouse itself is safe and secure. You can work with friends to make a simple tree platform on a low branch, or ask adults to help make something more substantial. You will need some lengths of wood, a hammer and nails, and someone with a basic plan in mind.

CAMOUFLAGE NET

TREEHOUSE TIPS

● Use a ladder to access the treehouse; can you work out how to pull it up to keep out enemy invaders?

● Make windows and spyholes as well as a door.

● How about dressing your treehouse? If it has little windows, add curtains to make it look more welcoming. Or you may wish to camouflage it from the outside world by covering it in a net threaded with leaves and twigs.

● Make a camp below your treehouse, perhaps with a home-made swing and a few log seats, to share with friends.

● Work out a way to lift up a basket loaded with a picnic or treats; this might be some rope thrown over a branch with a counterbalance on one end, or a more complicated pulley system.

TREEHOUSE IDEAS

TREE SWING

BASKET PULLEY

BALCONY VIEWPOINT

TREE LOOKOUT

FANTASY DENS

THEATRE AND STORYTELLING DENS

The wild world, with its fairy tales, myths and magic, is the perfect place to let your imagination run wild. Create spaces or dens for making-up new stories together, or for bringing favourite stories alive through puppet and theatre shows. Small dens might be good for puppet shows and story-telling, but larger tent-like structures or outdoor rooms (see pages 70–71 and 89-91) make wonderful theatres in a woodland clearing or a garden.

This clearing was the perfect spot for a play in which a wicked greedy lion with big ideas left the dry empty plains behind and went to live in a forest full of tasty creatures. But the forest fairies used tricks and magic to cast spells over the lion until he ran away with his tail between his legs, back to the plains where he belonged.

Theatre details You don't need to go and buy expensive costumes and props for your theatre; see what you can make using only natural and recycled materials.

Make-up Many tribal peoples traditionally decorated themselves with natural pigments. Try making face and body paints from mud, crushed chalk and squashed berries. Mix with a little water and then apply with a brush.

Safety tip Check that berries are safe to use and only collect mud from clean sources.

Natural crowns, hats and headdresses Cut strips of cardboard the right size to fit around your head. Stick double-sided tape to the cardboard and then decorate with leaves, grasses and other natural materials.

Costumes Thread leaves onto garden netting to make green camouflage capes in summer, or rich golden cloaks in autumn.

Props Look for natural materials that might become props to bring plays and stories alive; perhaps a discarded antler has magic powers, or a special stick can become a magic wand.

CAMOUFLAGE COSTUME

NATURAL FACE PAINT

GARDEN-NETTING CLOAK

MERMAID'S GROTTO

Perhaps this magical shell grotto was made by a real mermaid, working away over many years. Having been made by a mermaid, it is, of course, right at the bottom of the sea, so you will never be able to visit it, but perhaps these pictures may inspire you to make your own mermaid den.

Have a go at making a mermaid's retreat on a beach or in a cave, or make a grotto in a shed at home from shells and beach treasures collected on holiday. Avoid buying shells, as many of them are not collected sustainably. If you can't find enough, go and ask your local fish restaurant for some!

Safety tip Take great care when using a hot-glue gun (see page 50).

SHELL NECKLACE

MERMAID MAKE-UP AND JEWELS

MERMAID TREASURES

This mermaid's grotto is filled with special treasures.

- **Mermaid's dressing table** Make-up and jewels are stored in shell dishes on her sand-covered dressing table.

- **Shell-decorated hand mirror** A mirror tile and the frame of a hand mirror have been decorated with special shells, stuck on using hot glue.

- **Driftwood photo frame** Driftwood and shells glued together to make a frame for a photo of mermaid's best friends.

- **Jam jar nightlight** The grotto is lit lit with magical nightlights in jars with a layer of sand and some shells.

- **Shell Alice band** A pretty necklace and her Alice band have been decorated with shells.

- **Shell and driftwood mobile** Hang one from the doorway to warn off visitors or unwelcome intruders.

MERMAID'S DRESSING TABLE

SHELL-DECORATED HAND MIRROR

SHELL ALICE BAND

DRIFTWOOD PHOTO FRAME

JAM JAR NIGHTLIGHT

SHELL AND DRIFTWOOD MOBILE

MAGICAL TREE-ROOT DENS

Deep in the woods we discovered tangled, moss-covered tree roots, spreading snake-like across a steep bank.

Some of the earth beneath them had been washed away, leaving hidey-holes big enough to crawl into. What a perfect hideaway for woodland explorers; hidden in this earthy space, you can peep through the roots up into the green of the woodland canopy. Here you can become a wild woodland creature, a brave Hobbit or perhaps a dwarf from the underworld. Perhaps it's a magic den where the mossy roots will only protect you in their arms if you know the secret password.

This root chamber has been transformed into a wild woodland lair with leafy bunting, dream catchers, flying clay characters (see page 61), clay gargoyles and a cosy rug. Or perhaps a hollowed-out root chamber could become a fairy bower; look for a mossy stump to use as a throne for a fairy queen dressed with wings, a natural crown and a stick wand.

CLAY GARGOYLE

MOSSY THRONE

Twiggy wand This fairy wand was made from a long bendy stick folded at one end to make a star shape. Tie the loose end onto the stem. Decorate with flowers, feathers and seeds to add a touch of natural magic.

FAIRY CROWN AND WINGS

TWIGGY WAND

WOODLAND LAIR DETAILS

Natural bunting Make slits in the stems of leaves with a knife or a sharp stick and then thread the stems along some string. Alternatively, make a leaf chain just as you would make a daisy chain (page 34), or tie leaf stalks onto thread.

Fearsome faces and gargoyles Can you spot funny or scary faces hiding among the tangled roots? Perhaps you can bring them to life with a little clay, some chalk and a few woodland treasures to make eyes, noses, mouths and ears? Use whatever materials you think they need. Will they be fearsome enough to scare away unwanted intruders?

FAIRY BOWER DETAILS

Natural fairy crown Wind bendy stems into a circle (above left), making sure that it fits on your head. Weave in leaves and flowers.

Twiggy fairy wings Find some bendy green sticks and curve into wing shapes (above left). Tie together in the middle with string or raffia.

MINIATURE DENS FOR FAIRIES AND ELVES

Dens don't need to be lifesize. Perhaps you could create a pretty palace for a flower fairy, a secret cave for woodland elves or a twiggy tree house for cheeky pixies?

If you take care to make a welcoming doorway, whether it's a grand entrance or a little trap door at the top of a ladder, you never know who might move in! This fairy cottage (number 11) is made among mossy tree roots and designed to be hidden away yet offering a welcome to friendly folk in search of a new home. Make a fairy cottage and garden and wait to see who takes up residence. The challenge is to create a miniature woodland world by using only the natural materials around you, plus a little double-sided sticky tape and clay.

FAIRY COTTAGE DETAILS

- **Twig ladder** The fairy door is reached by a twig ladder stuck together with a little clay. The clay and twig windows have petal curtains.

- **Fairy banquet** A stone picnic table has been laid all ready for a banquet, with leaf plates, beechnut goblets and a snail-shell bowl. Beside the table, stone seats are covered in mossy cushions.

- **Leafy bunting** creates a real party feel. Cut leaves into triangles, then attach them to a twig with double-sided tape.

- **Swimming pool** There is even an inviting pool where fairies can swim among petals. Some fairies may choose to enter the water elegantly by the little ladder, while others like to make a big splash, diving in from the diving board.

- **Petal ballgown** Just in case a fairy has nothing new to wear, a beautiful ballgown, with feathers and a fashionable hat, lies ready waiting for the fairy ball.

TWIG AND CLAY LADDER

FAIRY BANQUET

SWIMMING POOL

LEAFY BUNTING

FAIRY DOOR

PETAL BALLGOWN

MINIATURE DENS FOR TOYS

Perhaps your toys would like the chance to enjoy a few den adventures of their own! Find a special place in the woods, park or garden or even among the plant pots on a patio or balcony. You could make a fort for toy action figures, a cosy shelter for a teddy bear or a special hideaway for your home-made toys.

Teddy-bear den Making dens on a miniature scale is a great way to practise making bigger dens! This teddy's woodland shelter was later used as a model for making a full-sized den.
Hideout for action toys Sheltering among tree roots under a big bracket fungus is a secret camp for toy soldiers. The trick to making really good toy dens is to take time and have fun creating all the little details; it can be helpful

ACTION-TOY HIDEOUT

LONG-NOSED GIRAFFE DEN

to take along some clay for sticking things together. An action-toy hideout might include an escape rope of woven grass, twiggy windows, ladders stuck together with clay (see page 52), bark doors and a comfy moss bed.

Dens for stick creatures A long-nosed giraffe (page 58) is quite at home in its tall stick and leaf shelter built against a wall.

MAKING TOYS FOR MINIATURE DENS

Try making little characters from the natural materials around you, such as sticks, grasses, leaves or fir cones. It might be handy to have some clay, string, scissors and sticky tape with you as well. Here are a few ideas for firing up your imagination:

TOYS FOR MINIATURE DENS

GRASS PEOPLE

TWIG WARRIOR

Grass people Using grass or thread, bind a bunch of grass together in the middle to make the body, and again a little further along to make a head, so that the grass ends form crazy hair. Split the lower half into two bunches and bind together to make legs. Bind a separate bunch to make arms, and push this through the middle of the body between the stems. Draw a face on a leaf, then stick it on with glue or tie it on with grass.

Clay and twig characters Mould a body out of clay and make it into a magical character with leafy wings, twig legs and perhaps nut or seed eyes and a mouth. Will it be fierce or friendly? Perhaps you could make a little warrior with bark armour and a bow and arrow, a flower fairy with leafy wings, or try transforming fir cones or conkers into little animals.

FIR-CONE ANIMALS

CLAY MAN

MONSTER DENS

Out there in the woods or the park, hidden monsters are biding their time, quietly watching, patiently waiting. The challenge is to spot them disguised among the trees. They may be friendly dragons, ancient dinosaurs, giant birds, enormous spiders or the craziest creatures of your wildest imagination.

Finding monster dens is all about discovering natural sculptures that offer places to hide, to play and to imagine. Some monsters may have been created with the help of human hands such as the dragon's nest and giant bird (below) offering its hollow belly as a woody throne. Other monster sculptures are entirely natural, just needing a beady eye to spot them, an active imagination to bring them alive and a brave explorer to discover their natural hiding places.

In this giant dinosaur (or dragon or lizard?) den (opposite), a long neck reaches up towards the trees and beside its front leg a hollow belly makes a natural den. This friendly lady dinosaur allowed children to climb all over her spiky back and crawl under her sheltering front leg, and was delighted when they gave her a stone eye and added fern fronds to make long eyelashes.

GIANT BIRD

DRAGON'S NEST AND EGG

Look for a quiet spot in the woods to discover animal shapes in the trees. Or make a giant nest like this dragon's nest with a huge egg waiting to hatch (can you hear the baby dragon wriggling around inside?)

STORAGE BOX BRICKS

BUILD UP WALLS

CHECK HEIGHT

WINTER WONDERLAND DENS

Even in the depths of winter there's lots of fun to be had making dens. Be sure to wrap up warm and wear good cosy, waterproof gloves, then get outdoors and have a go at making magical mid-winter igloos for you or your teddy bears, or miniature palaces and castles that are fit for an ice queen or king.

IGLOOS

Imagine living in a wintry world where the only building material is snow; this igloo made by warriors from the far north provided a base for feasts of warm bread and steaming soup, very welcome after sleigh adventures and snowball battles. Perhaps you would feel safer inside your igloo if it were to be guarded by a snowy dragon?

Make snow bricks by packing snow into plastic storage boxes (this won't work if the snow is very powdery). Tip the snow bricks out of the boxes and arrange them in a circle big enough for you and your friends to sit inside. Add a second layer of bricks on top of the first but slightly further in, towards the centre of the circle. Make sure the bricks in the second layer overlap the edges of the bricks in the first layer. Keep adding more layers of bricks,

moving in a little with each one. Pack loose snow into the gaps. Can you make the walls meet together at the top? You can always cheat and make a roof and door from bits of wood (cut some plywood if needs be). Place well-packed snow bricks around the inside to make seats, or just use the boxes as seats instead.

SNOWY MINI-DENS

Perhaps you could make a white palace for a snow queen, or a wintry city for tiny imaginary people? Place a snowy dragon on guard when you've finished!
Mini-igloo It's pretty tricky to make a lifesized igloo, so how about practising on a miniature igloo? Pack snow into little plastic containers to make bricks and build your igloo as described above. A perfect hidey hole for a teddy bear!

DOORWAY PEEPHOLE

SNOWY DRAGON
(WITH ICE TEETH)

MINI ICE QUEEN'S PALACE

Can you make a glistening ice fortress or palace suitable for an ice queen? Collect ice from broken puddles, the edges of a small stream, or leave bowls of water outside on a freezing cold night to make your own ice. Choose a special place to build; perhaps on a log, a tree stump or a rock. Fit the ice pieces together to make a palace or a fortress. Spraying cold water on to the ice should help the pieces stick together. Add sticks and stones to make it stronger if you wish, or perhaps use leaves covered in hoarfrost to decorate.

You could also try to make a wintry outdoor area to go with the palace. How about creating an ice rink by surrounding some ice from a puddle with a miniature wall of snow?

MINIATURE IGLOO

MINI ICE-QUEEN PALACE

JUNK DENS

OUTDOOR PLAYSPACES

Find a safe space in the city, perhaps at an adventure playground, an after-school club or maybe in the park, in the garden or on the terrace at home. Collect unwanted everyday objects; can you re-imagine and recreate them into fantastic playspaces, dens and forts?

Work with your friends to design and build your own space, somewhere to be free and to have fun. But remember that dens are not permanent, and the best way to improve your designing and building skills is to destroy and rebuild.

Forts and hideaways really can be made anywhere, from almost anything. In this adventure playground, anything goes! Amazing dens have been made from wooden pallets, plastic bread baskets, water containers (they make great drums!), hardboard, car tyres, old furniture and carpets. All sorts of things that have been thrown away may have another use if you apply some imagination.

Some structures, such as a two-storey den, will need a little adult help in order to make them sturdy and safe. Make dens more welcoming by painting the walls in bright colours, making windows or doorways from old blinds and adding some old furniture and carpet offcuts. Junk dens can be anything you want them to be, from a playhouse or a palace to a space rocket or perhaps a launch pad (see page 72), perfect for leaping onto the big squidgy mat below.

OUTDOOR ROOM

To make rooms outdoors, you need to define the space by creating some walls. This room in the shelter of a tree (below opposite) has walls made from pallets and hardboard. It is furnished with old chairs, tables, wood offcuts, plastic crates and other bits and pieces. An outdoor room is a perfect place for making a lot of mess and having fun; there's no need to worry about spilling paint when there's no carpet to ruin! If the grownups don't like the mess, screen off the den with some old fabric, or build something stronger out of old trellis.

PAINT YOUR DEN

OUTDOOR PLAYSPACE TIPS

• When collecting materials, make sure that you only gather up items that are no longer wanted.

• Some of the items may be large and you may need help to construct safe dens; but the design should be yours!

• Ever wanted to draw on the walls? Paint hardboard or pallet walls with blackboard paint so you can chalk messages and pictures all over them if you wish!

IDEAS

STURDY FRAME STRUCTURE

WELCOME

LAUNCH PAD

WATER-CONTAINER DRUMS

TWO-STOREY DEN

PLASTIC-BOTTLE DENS

Have you ever noticed how many plastic bottles and plastic containers get thrown away? Perhaps you could put some to good use by transforming them into a den, a playspace or a greenhouse.

GREENHOUSE DEN

Perhaps it's a playhouse in winter and a greenhouse in summer! You will need about 40 long garden canes and lots of plastic bottles. Cut the bottoms off most of the bottles, and remove the tops. Push a garden cane into a complete bottle. Now push several cut bottles down the cane until the bottles thread all the way along. Do the same with all the other canes, using coloured bottles if you wish. Work with an adult to make a wooden frame for the bottles on canes to fit into (below). Add a roof of corrugated plastic, or more bottles on canes.

THREADED PLASTIC BOTTLES

PLASTIC-BOTTLE DEN TIPS

What other ideas can you come up with?

● **Plastic-bottle tent** Arrange plastic bottles on canes (left), but fix the rows of bottles together with hot glue to make two panels. Lean the panels towards each other to make a tent shape, gluing them along the ridge to secure. Take care if using a glue gun.

● **Junk igloo** Use plastic milk cartons for bricks. Make a circle of cartons on the ground, sticking them together with hot glue. Build up layers, as you would for a winter ice igloo (see page 64).

STAND BOXES IN CASTLE SHAPE

FIX BOXES BY GLUING CARD JOINTS

LIFTING DRAWBRIDGE

ARROW SLIT

CARDBOARD CASTLES

Can you imagine having a real cardboard castle, a place to defend from enemies, to hold prisoners and share banquets?

This castle, with crenellated towers and turrets, a working drawbridge, portcullis, arrow slits and pennant flags, provides a play space for hours of imaginary games. Inside there are doors leading into little rooms inside each tower, and a big space to share with friends.

  This is a great team project to share with family and friends. Don't let anyone in the household throw away big boxes; store them in a garage or shed until you have enough. If you can't collect enough boxes at home, see if the neighbours are throwing any out on recycling day, or ask for boxes at a garden centre or a furniture store. Then, using a hot glue gun, a good craft knife and lots of imagination, you can make a fabulous castle. Choose a sunny day when the ground is dry so there's no risk of your cardboard becoming soggy and soft.

CASTLE DETAILS

Building the basic structure Start off by making the front of your castle; our structure included a big tower on each side, with an entrance in the middle. These towers were made from two

identical boxes turned inside out, so no writing is visible. A large, flatter, box was fixed between the towers using hot glue and braced with smaller pieces of card, also stuck on with hot glue as shown on page 74. Arched doorways were cut carefully in the centre of each side of this box; the outer door was left attached at the bottom. Another wall was made behind the towers to create a space large enough for several people to fit in. Little doors were made from inside the castle and leading into each tower, to create two small rooms (or perhaps they were more likely to be dungeons!).

Drawbridge The outer door, still attached to the bottom of the box, became the drawbridge. A knotted rope was pulled through a small hole cut near the top of the loose door. The two doors were then stuck together, with the knotted rope end sandwiched between them. A small hole was made above the outer archway and the rope was threaded through it, ready to be used for raising and lowering the drawbridge. The challenge was to raise it fast enough to keep out all those marauding enemies (see page 74).

Internal decoration Have fun decorating the castle by drawing fireplaces, family portraits or suits of armour directly on to the internal walls. Add a real rug or carpet on the floor, a small wooden table and perhaps some goblets and a plate of food so you can enjoy a lavish feast, secure inside your stronghold.

Safety tips Take care when using a hot glue gun. Only use a craft knife and staple gun with adult help and see Tool Safety Guidelines on page 140 for more advice.

ADD FURNITURE AND FEASTS

Crenellations Carefully cut these out on long strips of card using a craft knife. Cut out a square of card first, then use that piece to measure roughly where to cut the rest of the crenellations.

Portcullis Cut several cardboard strips and stick them together in a mesh formation. Paint it black, then stick it on behind the doorway. This portcullis did not raise and lower but looked effective; why not try to design one that works?

Arrow slits Cut a few slits in the castle walls so you can spy on the enemies and fire your arrows at them.

Turrets Roll a large piece of flexible card into a long tube. These turrets were attached to the castle using a long piece of wood to strengthen them; the wood protruded from the bottom of the turret so it could be stapled securely to the sides of the tower. You can add crenellations to the turrets, or make a pointed roof from a large semicircle of card folded it into a cone.

Pennant flags These are most effective if made from brightly coloured, lightweight fabric. Cut very long, thin, triangle shapes and hot-glue them onto garden canes or sticks.

DECORATE THE WALLS

CARDBOARD TENT DENS

This cardboard tent over a bamboo frame is smaller and easier to make than a huge castle.

This temporary shelter on the desert planet Tattooine provided a place to hide from Tusken Raiders.

● Tape bamboo canes together to make a sturdy frame. Make any shape you like; this one is a typical tent shape, but its triangular roof creates more room inside.

● Flatten cardboard boxes into panels and hot-glue them to the frame.

● Clear plastic water bottles make wonderful windows. Cut the top and bottom off a bottle and flatten the middle out into a flat panel. Glue several panels together to make larger windows.

● The bottle bases make great spy holes. Draw round the base of a bottle on the cardboard walls and then cut out the circle with a craft knife (with adult help). Replace the bottle bottom back into the hole, securing it in place with hot glue.

Safety tip Take care when using hot glue guns.

BAMBOO CANE FRAME

DECORATE WITH HANDPRINTS & CAPS

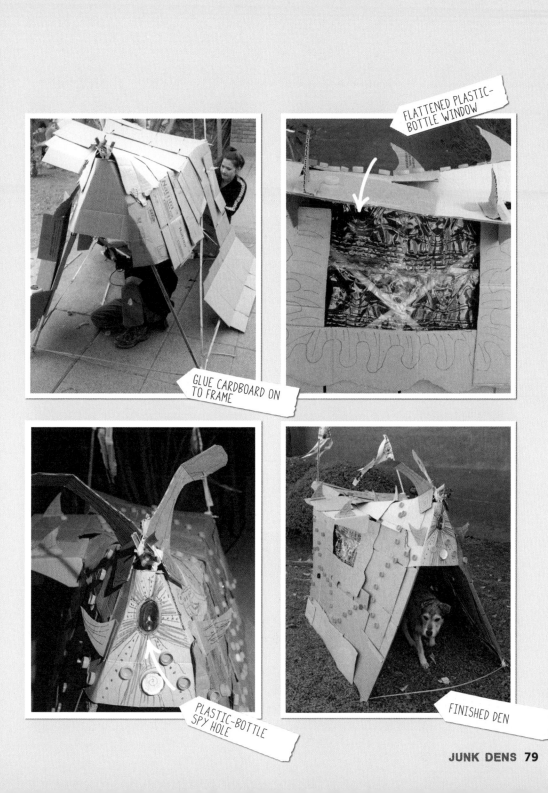

FLATTENED PLASTIC-BOTTLE WINDOW

GLUE CARDBOARD ON TO FRAME

PLASTIC-BOTTLE SPY HOLE

FINISHED DEN

JUNK PARTY DENS

Try the junk party den challenge! What sort of den can you make from discarded wrapping paper, packaging and the contents of the recycling bin?

Transform old packaging or the contents of the recycling bin into a great futuristic space pod, all set for lift off. Next, make some junk space costumes from newspapers, plastic bags, bin liners and bottles to create outfits that are worthy of Darth Vader, James Bond or brave knights.

HOW TO MAKE A SPACE-POD DEN

You will need eight bendy sticks; hazel and willow are ideal. Push the sticks into the ground in a circle, bending the sticks over to meet each other to make a series of overlapping arches. Fix a clear plastic storage box over the top using strong tape, to make a lookout. Completely cover the stick frame with bubblewrap, fixed in place with tape, but leave a doorway to one side. Decorate the pod with a selection of junk such as foil food containers, plastic caps and perhaps an old keyboard as a control panel.

JUNK ASTRONAUT SUIT

TINFOIL SPACE HELMET

Junk space costumes
All you need now is a couple of astronauts complete with tinfoil space helmets, armed with space guns and light sabres, made out of junk of course!

SLEEPOUTS & PARTIES

SLEEPOUT DENS

For a real adventure, sleep outside in a den on a warm summer's night. Whether you're in the garden or in a field, listen to the sounds of nature as the sun sets, or to the dawn chorus when the early morning light wakes you. If the weather is warm and dry, don't worry about waterproofing your den, apart from a groundsheet to keep damp away.

GARDEN SLEEPOUT DEN

A washing-line den (see page 32) is great for a garden sleepout; you can always dash back indoors if the weather changes, or if you feel anxious in the middle of the night! Transform the den into a magical retreat with a few glow sticks and a string of fairy lights. Perhaps you could stage a shadow puppet show (see page 46) or shine a bright torch onto the sheet to see how many moths are attracted?

HOW TO MAKE A DIY TENT

This simple DIY tent keeps out the rain and provides a great place for sleeping out with friends. You will need a large waterproof cover (a tarp or a big sheet of plastic), some rope or cord, some tent pegs (see page 135), a groundsheet and two 2m/7ft sturdy sticks. You may also need some adult help.

● Find a good place for your tent, preferably on open, level ground. Sharpen one end of each stick before pushing them into the ground about 2–3m/7–10ft apart, depending on the size of your waterproof cover.

● Ask someone to hold each stick firmly while you fasten a length of rope between them to make a ridge. Using tent pegs, attach two guy ropes from each stick and secure them firmly in place, making sure the ridge rope is taut.

● Slide the plastic sheeting over the ridge until there is the same amount of material on each side. Attach short guy ropes (see page 135) and secure with tent pegs.

● Use a waterproof groundsheet to guarantee a good night's sleep!

PEG THE GUY ROPES TO SUPPORT THE TENT POLES

PEG OUT PLASTIC SHEET

FINISHED TENT

LEAF-SHELTER DEN

This carefully designed shelter will keep you snug as a bug all night long! You may need adult help with moving heavy logs and with building; you wouldn't want your shelter collapsing on you during the night!

STICK WALLS

HOW TO BUILD A MADE-TO-MEASURE, ONE-PERSON, LEAF-SHELTER DEN

● Find a level spot beside a forked tree. Make sure there are no standing dead trees nearby, as they can be dangerous on a windy night. Brush away sticks, stones and leaves to make a smooth surface. Look for three long, straight sticks, each one about 1m/3ft taller than you.

● To make the shelter's frame, place the end of one stick into the tree fork, so the stick is at an angle over the sleeping area. Put the other sticks on the ground beside it as shown. Lie down to check the shelter frame is exactly your size.

● Arrange shorter sticks all the way along each side of the shelter (left, middle), leaving a gap near the tree on one side as the entrance. Place the sticks close together, making sure the top of each stick rests on the ridgepole.

● Collect armfuls of dry, crispy leaves from the woodland floor. Starting at ground level, cover the shelter in a deep thatch of leaves.

LEAF COVERING

LARGE LEAF-SHELTER

BREWING TEA

This is the trick to keeping you warm and dry, so make sure you do a good job! Place some dry leaves on the floor of the shelter to make a soft mattress. When you are ready for bed, push your sleeping bag into the shelter and then squirm inside your cosy, sweet-scented cocoon.

To create more adventure, make a small firepit outside your shelter to heat up supper, warm you up and keep insects away. Make the fire small and safe, and burn it down to ashes before bedtime (see Fire Safety Guidelines on page 140).

A LEAF SHELTER TO SHARE WITH FRIENDS

If you aren't brave enough to sleep in a shelter on your own, make a bigger version that you can then share with friends. Choose a good spot, near to fallen trees, that gives you access to plenty of places on which to lean several ridge poles. Make the shelter in a similar way to the small shelter above, but, if the weather is dry, it need not be waterproof.

OUTDOOR PARTY DEN

Taking the indoors outdoors is a magical way to celebrate a birthday, a family party, a midsummer evening or to put on some outdoor theatre (see page 46). Create a 'room' in the garden, at the park, in the woods or on a riverbank, adding indoor details to create some unexpected magic. But be sure to get permission to take the indoors out, in dry weather.

WILD OUTDOOR ROOM

This woodland glade, with its rustic table and log stools, is perfect for an outdoor dining hall for a summer banquet. These tips will help you make your own wild outdoor room.

● Choose a defined space in the woods, the park or the garden; the space should be room-sized, and although it doesn't need to be totally enclosed,

OUTDOOR LIVING ROOM

PICTURE FRAME & FAMILY PHOTOS

it should be clearly defined by trees, bushes or a pile of sticks.

● This woodland clearing becomes a room as soon as it is furnished with a standard lamp, an armchair and colourful cushions on log stools. But extra details such as candlesticks, family photos, a picture frame and a vase on a log side table make it feel like home.

● The log table has natural details of leaf place mats, bark plates and a huge bark fruit bowl, lined with giant leaves.

● After dark, the room will be lit by a wild chandelier. This is made by hanging night-lights in jars and glass candle holders from a long stick that is suspended by rope across the gap between two trees. The jars have string or wire tied around the top so they can be easily attached.

● Choose indoor things that fit with whatever magical setting you are trying to create; perhaps an old deep-pile rug, or strings of leaf bunting and pictures hanging from the trees.

● Enjoy your outdoor party! And don't forget to take all the indoor things back inside when the party is over.

BARK AND LEAF PLATES

JAR LANTERN ON WILD CHANDELIER

INDOOR CAMPING

Camping in the woods is great when the weather is fine, but the grownups definitely won't want to sleep outdoors if it's pouring with rain! To avoid disappointment, try to bring the outdoors in, and set up camp indoors, in an imaginary woodland. Perhaps you could pack a bag and set off for a wet adventure in the wilds of the garden or the remote regions of the park before returning to the 'wild living room' forest?

Pitch your tent indoors by tying some guy ropes to furniture or door handles. Extend the guy ropes with extra string if need be. Weigh down the edges of the tent with books or doorstops. Bring some greenery indoors to create a leafy forest glade, and bring it to life with a few toy birds or soft toy animals. Create a fake campfire in front of the tent, complete with logs, paper and cellophane flames lit by a torch, then make your tent cosy with sleeping mats, sleeping bags and pillows. Enjoy some campout food round the fire; perhaps corn on the cob and sausages, followed by marshmallows.

When it's cold and wet outside, create a really cosy campout indoors and simply pretend that you are out in the wild. Either pitch a tent indoors, or make your own den under the table and gather around a fake campfire, to complete the illusion of the wild outdoors.

INDOOR SLEEPOUT

SPOOKY HALLOWEEN DEN

For a thrilling outdoor Halloween, make a spooky den in the woods or create a scary room in the garden. Invite your witch and wizard friends to fly in on home-made broomsticks after dark (if they are brave enough, of course) to bob for a few apples, cook up spells and enjoy a pumpkin pie feast.

Instead of buying lots of gaudy plastic Halloween props from the store, have some fun making spooky and amusing items from natural materials collected in the woods or the garden.

Look outside in the park or your garden for a special place in which to make a scary den. Can you find monster-like trees with low, twisted branches or secret caves deep inside dark bushes or hedges or even a hideaway under a table on the patio? Or out in the woods, try propping some fallen sticks against a branch to make a lean-to den, then decorate it with scary natural details. This den is protected by snakes emerging from broken branches and a leafy spider over the doorway. Perhaps you could add eyes to a few nearby trees, transforming them into tree monsters? For a real Halloween adventure, visit your den after dark with pumpkin or paper-bag lanterns, friends and a picnic.

USE PUMPKIN LID TO MAKE A HEAD

Decorate a pumpkin Hollow out a pumpkin and cut out eyes and a mouth to make a glowing lantern. An easier way to make a scary or friendly pumpkin face is to stick on leaves for the eyes, mouth and ears. Use the pumpkin stalk as a nose. No cutting involved!

Safety tips Get adult help when using knives to cut pumpkins. Only use night-lights when with an adult.

SCARY DETAILS

Witch's hat, wand and broomstick
Whittle and carve a small twisted stick
for a wand. A larger stick with bunches
of twigs attached with string can become
a broomstick. To make the hat, twist
a semi-circle of black card into a cone;
check it fits, then fix with tape. Decorate
with leafy scary faces and bats.

Leaf spiders and bats Stick eight twigs
on a leaf with double-sided tape, add
some berry eyes and hang from a string.
Alternatively make a spider's body from
a fir cone or a lump of clay, and then
add legs and scary eyes. Make bats in
the same way, using leaves for wings.

Leaf-face lantern Cut out scary
Halloween faces on coloured leaves to
decorate your den or outdoor room.
Or attach faces around jam jars or
clear plastic pots with rubber bands
to make lanterns for night lights.

Spooky paper-bag lantern For best
effect, use bags with handles. Cut out
scary faces and decorate them with leaves
and seeds. Place a torch or a glow-stick in
each bag to create a spooky glow.

Terrifying stick monsters Just add
clay and natural materials to make the
scariest creatures!

Batty bunting Cut bats out of sycamore
or maple leaves, and use a large needle
to thread them along strings.

WITCH'S HAT

LEAF SPIDER

SPOOKY PAPER-BAG LANTERN

LEAF-FACE LANTERN

TERRIFYING STICK MONSTER

BATTY BUNTING

STRAW-BALE PARTY DENS

A few straw bales and planks are ideal for building garden dens. This is a fun project for a party or for a group of friends; the bales are heavy to move, so teamwork is definitely required. Perhaps you could build a pirate ship complete with pirate flag, a fort for a knight or a castle for a princess. Try changing the design to make different dens, or split into two teams and build straw-bale camps. Perhaps the teams could try to capture each other's dens, with the help of flour bomb ammunition.

HOW TO MAKE A STRAW-BALE DEN

First find your bales; there are various suppliers on the Internet or try contacting a local farmer. Stack bales carefully as you build. Make sure the bales in each layer overlap the bales below them. For safety, don't build the bales very high. Leave gaps in a few places to make doors, windows or tunnels to crawl through. Use long planks or perhaps a tarp to make a roof or floor.

Safety tip Build carefully; bales are heavy and you don't want one to fall on top of you while you are constructing your den.

PLANK RAMP

FLOUR BOMBS

Plank ramp Try using planks to make sloping ramps for a skateboard ride or use planks or ladders to link the dens.

Flour bombs Put a spoonful of flour onto a sheet of paper towel. Pull the paper around the flour and twist the ends tightly together.

NATURAL DENS

BEACH DRIFTWOOD DENS

How about hunting for driftwood on the beach or sticks from nearby woodland and designing your own little shelter? It might be a place to play or to spy from, a shelter from the wind and rain, or perhaps it's a shady retreat in which to read a book on a hot sunny day. Do a little beachcombing and collect treasures left behind by the retreating tide; useful den-making objects might include string to tie things together, plastic boxes to make seats or tables, and perhaps feathers or seaweed for finishing touches.

Find a structure to build your den around, or dig out a hollow in the sand and then make a stick-style tepee over the hollow. You could mark out a little territory around the den with sticks or stones, perhaps in a pattern. Finish your shelter with a grass flag, seashell decorations and perhaps a throne ready to welcome Neptune.

DRIFTWOOD CREATURES

Driftwood often forms amazing shapes and patterns, all carved and worn over time by the relentless pounding of the sea. If you look carefully, you might discover faces of sea monsters hidden in the wood. In this driftwood den (opposite and right), a sea serpent and a deer's head protect the den and scare away intruders.

TEPEE-STYLE DRIFTWOOD DEN

NEPTUNE'S DRIFTWOOD THRONE

DRIFTWOOD DEER WITH ANTLERS

LIVING-WOOD DRAGON

If you look very carefully in your local woodland, perhaps you will spot the biggest dragon ever, lurking among the trees. Hazel the dragon tempts passers-by to venture deeper into this particular woodland so they can play and explore.

She is waiting for warriors armed with wooden swords to protect her from her enemies and to make a den deep inside her tummy, clamber over her tail or share a picnic beneath her legs. And she may even let the bravest adventurers climb high up onto her back, to fly away with her over the treetops.

This beautiful dragon is a very rare beast, created one winter by a skilled woodland artist. He wove stems of living hazel together to create Hazel's massive, muscled body, legs and tail. Every springtime she grows new leafy scales, which turn golden in the autumn before they are shed again, in preparation for winter's hibernation.

You may not find a dragon such as this, but look carefully, and you may find your own living dragons in the woods (see page 63). Help them emerge from hiding by creating a long tail and legs with sticks, eyes from stones or even fiery breath from red leaves, Or can you create a dragon's lair deep in the forest?

Safety tip Always take care if climbing on natural structures.

DRAGON DETAILS

Baby dragons Look for a suitable dragon stick, add a clay head and then natural wings, eyes, ears and fiery breath. Can you make a double-headed dragon, a dragon with fierce prickly holly wings or a dragon hobby horse?

Dragon nests Twist stems and twigs together and then decorate with leaves and hide them among the undergrowth. And don't forget to look out for some dragon eggs!

Storytelling The belly of a dragon or monster is the perfect place in which to share stories and dragon tales together.

DRAGON'S HEAD

DEN INSIDE DRAGON'S BELLY

DRAGON'S BACK LOOKOUT

DRAGON IDEAS

DRAGON WITH PRICKLY WINGS

GUARDING AGAINST ENEMIES

LARGE STICK DRAGON

BABY CLAY DRAGON

HEDGEROW HIDEAWAY

Big, old hedgerows can provide a secret shadowy world for hiding in.
This hedgerow hideaway has been lovingly furnished with a hammock,
a chair cut from a log and a comfy tyre swing seat hanging from a branch.

The cheerful decorations include strings of flags and bunting made from brightly coloured plastic bags cut into diamond shapes and stapled over garden twine. Meanwhile, create a lookout post for surveying enemy invaders by placing two ladders poking up above the hedge.

There are several entrances, but the favourite one involves squirming through an old tyre (see page 136). A blackboard hatch with hinges lifts up to reveal a secret spyhole. It can also be used to display warning messages to enemies or invitations to friends. There are even handy places to hang up coats.

The creators of this den love to use it every day because it's their very own secret space, with small, child-size entrances, little passages to explore and

OLD TYRE SWING

HOME-MADE PLASTIC-BAG BUNTING

places to climb up into the branches. Grownups are occasionally invited to visit, but we think they aren't too keen on squeezing through the narrow entrances.

MAKE YOUR OWN HEDGEROW HIDEAWAY

If you have a hedge or some dense bushes in your garden, look for a hollow space deep inside, which could be just perfect for a den. You may need to cut back a few branches, carve out the middle, or even make a tunnel to gain access to it. But try to make sure that your hideaway is completely invisible from the outside, so it will be all the better for when you want to host super-secret pow-wows and gatherings!

BLACKBOARD FOR MESSAGES

HAMMOCK BED

DENS INSIDE BUSHES AND TREES

Some bushes and trees harbour secret spaces waiting to be transformed into magical dens and hideaways. Here, you can disappear into an imaginary world or become a wild creature, tucked away in your lair.

Perhaps an old tree such as a twisted willow may have a hollow big enough for you to crawl inside. You might find a tree with branches hanging right down to the ground, that offers a green haven within a swishing skirt of dangling leaves. Or you might discover some rambling, tangled old bushes that invite you to crawl deep inside to find a perfectly hidden refuge.

RHODODENDRON DEN

The dark, twisting branches of the evergreen shrub rhododendron often spread out over a large area, offering many hidey-holes. This bush provides the perfect starting point to create a woodland play space. Take favourite toys to the den and create an outdoor playroom, perhaps with a shelf for toys and books and a table laid for a tea party with friends. Explore the spaces among the branches, or cover the floor with a cosy rug for magical storytelling with granny.

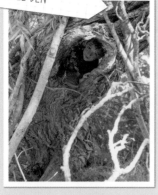

HOLLOW TREE DEN

DOORBELL

Make an entrance
To create an inviting entranceway, you could use some bendy sticks to make an arched doorway, then cover it with leafy greenery. Finish it off by hanging up a bell; a great way to invite guests in or warn away intruders!

DENS FOR WILDLIFE SPYING

Natural dens provide perfect windows onto nature. Hidden away in a shelter among trees and bushes, beside a river, pond or lake or even in a garden, you can share in the secret world of wild creatures. Can you spot insects, birds or even shy mammals? Try to be very quiet and look closely at everything that's going on around you.

MAKING A WILDLIFE HIDE

Small natural dens make great wildlife hides, but for best results follow these tips. Choose a quiet spot away from busy paths and in a good place for seeing wildlife, perhaps near a river or pond, or beside an animal pathway. If making a garden hide, put it beside a pond, near some bird feeders or close to plants with flowers or berries visited by insects or birds.

Wildlife hides must blend with the surroundings; use natural materials from the area, a camouflage net or some cloth or a tarp of the right colour. Make

sure your hide does not stick up above the skyline. Follow nature's example and avoid too many straight lines! Make sure there are little holes you can peep through, perhaps just big enough for you to look through with binoculars. To test how good your hide is, walk away from it and then turn around and look back at it; how easy is it to see?

WILDLIFE WATCHING TIPS

Here are a few tips to increase your chances of spotting wildlife. For best results go out in the faded light of early morning or evening. You will need to be very still and try to 'disappear'; wear warm comfy clothes and opt for natural green and brown colours. You could be in for a long wait, so make yourself comfy with a groundsheet, cushions and blankets. Take along some quiet snacks; avoid crunchy crisps or sweets with noisy wrappers!

To disappear into nature, make yourself a special camouflage outfit using materials found near your hide. If your outfit hides your human shape, you may not need a hide because you will be wearing your very own no-hide hide!

• Cover a long strip of cardboard with double-sided tape and then curve it round to fit your head like a crown. Completely cover the sticky tape in leaves, grasses and other locally found natural materials.

• Make a camouflage cape by pushing bunches of grass and leaves through garden netting bought at a garden centre.

• Disguise your face with clay, mud or green face paint.

MEADOW DEN

Lying quietly in a meadow hideaway on a summer's day is perhaps the best way to be totally immersed in wild summertime. Peep through the long, slender grass stems, golden buttercups and cow parsley that looks like summer snowflakes. Smell crushed grass and listen to birds singing and insects buzzing. On a summer's day, a meadow hideaway or fairy bower provides a special sanctuary; somewhere to read a book, paint a picture, become a flower fairy or share a picnic with friends.

MAKING A MEADOW DEN
The best time to make meadow dens is in early to mid-summer when the grass has grown long but hasn't yet been cut for silage or hay. First, choose

your location; perhaps a field, a grassy woodland edge or long grass at the edge of a park. Always seek permission to go there and only use a small area for your den. Meadows are precious places for wildflowers, butterflies, beetles, birds and small mammals, so it's best to leave most of the grasses and flowers growing naturally. Perhaps you could plan ahead and have your own meadow at home? Just persuade the adults to let an area of grass grow long enough to become a lovely place to play, and a haven for wildlife. Look for an area where the grasses and flowers are tall enough to hide in. Make a series of arches with a few bendy sticks pushed into the ground, then weave grasses and flowers growing nearby through the arches. Flatten a small area under the arches just big enough to sit or lie. Try twisting grasses together to make windows, as on opposite page. Furnish your den with a rug or a log table, but take them home with you when you leave.

MEADOW DEN DETAILS

Make a buttercup crown by twisting stems together. Make a flower chain (see page 34) or some grass dolls (see page 60). How many different grasses do you think you can spot?

GRASS MEADOW PEOPLE

DISCOVER A MINIATURE WORLD

Grass meadow people
Twist living grasses to make tiny people.
Natural discovery
Crawl through the grass to find a bustling miniature world with a magnifying glass; can you imagine how huge the plants must seem to the tiny creatures?

COLLECTOR'S MUSEUM DEN

The natural world is a great place for finding fascinating bits and pieces such as birds' skulls, pine cones, eggshells and feathers.

You may enjoy digging up archaeological treasures such as old pottery, or discovering geology via rocks and fossils. Your precious collections may not be wanted indoors, especially if they include anything a bit gruesome like a bird's wing, a fox's foot or an owl pellet, so set up a mini-museum in an old shed or a garden den. The treasures in this garden-shed museum include an old wasp's nest, a snakeskin, a bird's skull, a mermaid's purse, prize-winning conkers, a pheasant's wing and plaster of Paris dinosaur footprints!

SCAVENGER COLLECTION

CREATING A MUSEUM

Try to record what you find and where you find it, perhaps in a notebook or nature diary, or label individual exhibits for your visitors.

• Use boxes, baskets and shelves to display treasures for your friends and family. Decide how to sort each collection, perhaps by type, by size, by colour or by shape.

• Compile a museum quiz and ask visitors to guess what everything is! Encourage visitors to handle the exhibits.

• Keep looking out for new finds to update your museum collections, or you could even offer special seasonal exhibitions.

• Create a lending museum, by making your exhibits available for decorating dens (see Garden-table Den on pages 36-7), providing props for outdoor plays (see pages 70-72) or inspiring some storytelling.

CAVE DEN

For thousands of years, human beings have used caves as shelters, often decorating them with paintings. A fire in this cave was used to warm its new inhabitants after a chilly swim. They decorated it so it became their own special place to enjoy during a family beach holiday.

CAVE DECORATING

Use stones from the beach to draw patterns and designs of creatures you have seen at the seaside, or to tell a story through pictures, like the mermaid (below) who made friends with a dolphin with big teeth. Use a bucket of water to paint on temporary designs and beach graffiti; remember to take a picture of your cave art before it disappears from view. Or experiment with ways of leaving handprints on the rocks or sand, just like ancient peoples would have done.
Safety tip Many caves are only exposed at low tide, so always check tide tables.

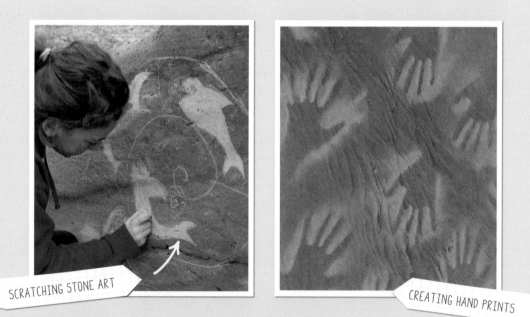

SCRATCHING STONE ART

CREATING HAND PRINTS

PLANT YOUR OWN LIVING DEN

Making a living den is a great family project. Plant in early spring and see your lattice turn into a wonderful hideaway.

MAKING A LIVING WILLOW DOME

● You will need lots of long, straight rods of bendy willow (not crack willow or weeping willow); see Internet for suppliers. Always use the willow rods within a week of being cut. You also need secateurs, some compost and cable ties or string, to tie the rods together.

● Place your den in a light space that's not too dry. Decide on the size by making an arch of willow to measure how wide the circle should be. Draw a circle on the ground, then dig a trench round the circle and fill it with compost. Push the willow rods about 10in/25cm into the ground around the circle, leaving a gap for the door.

● Bend two willow rods on opposite sides of the circle towards each other to make an arch; twist and tie them together. Do this all around the circle until you have a dome. Push shorter rods into the ground beside each larger rod, tying them in at at an angle to make a lattice, as shown, to strengthen the dome. Your dome will burst into life in the spring. Thread new growth back into the lattice.

WILLOW RODS IN A CIRCLE

TIE RODS TOGETHER TO SECURE

MAKE LATTICE TO IMPROVE STRENGTH

DEN TIPS

What are the key ingredients for making great dens? We think you need lots of imagination, a good location, some building materials and friends to work with. Our *Going Wild* top den tips will help you build sturdy shelters, have fun and stay safe.

BUILDING TIPS

The dens in this book are all about having fun outdoors while looking after wild places. These tips and the safety guidelines on pages 140-1 will help you stay safe.

● Only make dens in safe places. Don't make them under dead trees, too near water, beside a busy road... you get the picture.

● Only make dens where you have permission to do so; don't use the best flowerbeds in the garden or the neatly trimmed hedge at the park.

● Make sure a grownup knows where you are and what you are doing.

● Build carefully; do you really want your den to collapse on top of you?

● Choose den-building materials that are strong and safe. It's best not to use very heavy branches, rotten branches, thorny sticks or bunches of stinging nettles. If building a den from old junk (see pages 68-81), don't use glass or wood with nails sticking out of it.

● Be careful turning around when moving long branches; your friends won't appreciate being bashed on the head or knocked over.

● Never leave litter behind. It's OK to leave a natural den in place, but remember it may not be quite the same when you go back!

● Take care when using knives and homemade weapons, making fires or making dens near water; check out the safety guidance on page 140.

● Always look after wild places wherever they are; don't damage living trees and plants. Care for them so they will continue to be there to care for you in the future.

BE PREPARED

So, you are off to the woods, the garden or the adventure playground to make a den. What will you need?

- Wear comfy old clothes. If it's wet outside or you are going somewhere a bit overgrown, wear waterproof outerwear or dungarees.
- Thick gardening gloves in case of prickles or stings.
- Stuff for tying and fixing things together.
- Things to use as a roof and to cover the ground.
- Enough den rations to feed and water the den-building workers or to prepare a mini-feast to enjoy in your completed den.

CONSTRUCTION TIPS

Be aware of what's around you and watch out for natural hazards; a den under a low branch is great, but don't bang your head.

Come prepared with a range of equipment so you are ready to make the most of all den-building opportunities.

WHERE TO BUILD YOUR DEN

It's all about location, location, location!

Choose a spot that is dry and flat, on higher ground; it may be dry when you make your den, but you don't want to wake up in a puddle if it rains!

Never make dens in or near standing dead trees that might fall on you and don't make dens in trees that have dead branches.

If you have a garden or backyard, ask for your own space for den building (see page 27); you are likely to spend more time in the garden than the grownups, so why shouldn't you have your own space? At the park, find den spaces beside trees, among bushes or on play equipment.

In the garden You could make dens under the washing line, in an old shed, under the play equipment, inside a hedge or perhaps you have the perfect tree for a treehouse.

In the woods Look out for fallen tree trunks, hollow trees, space under low branches or in between the roots of a fallen tree, like in the picture above.

Ready-made dens Look for natural features that offer den-like hiding places or shelters. Also try to seek out someone else's abandoned den and personalize it.

BUILDING MATERIALS

Try to use what is free and look for loose materials in the woods, in the shed, or just lying around. But remember, don't take what isn't yours to take.

Recycled items are great for junk dens made from from old pallets, tyres, crates, bread boxes and plastic water bottles, as well as hardboard and cardboard boxes.

Building a garden den? Use a garden table, a trampoline or climbing frame, goal posts, planks, garden trellis, deckchairs or garden clippings, such as branches and leaves.

Building poles can be made from long, fallen sticks, bendy sticks of hazel or willow, garden canes, tent poles or even recycled broom handles.

Tent-style dens need a sturdy ridge of sticks or rope as a backbone. Wedge a strong stick in the Y-shape made between a tree trunk and a branch.

If you can't find trees with conveniently placed branches, then wedge a long, Y-shaped stick between tree trunks to support a ridge instead.

Another option you can try is to wedge a long stick between two trees growing very close together, perhaps using smaller sticks to wedge it in place, as shown here.

If making a rope ridge between two trees, always make sure the rope is pulled very tight and then tied securely round each tree with good, strong knots.

Cover your den with sticks and leaves, camouflage nets, old sheets, tarps, large plastic sheets, cardboard or even old plywood or a plastic corrugated sheet.

A great way to make a natural roof or wall is to build a lattice of sticks and then cover it with a thatch of grasses or leaves to create a really cosy space inside.

Dens that include several individual rooms can be much more fun to play in, so try to make some dividing walls using materials such as sticks, tarps or old sheets.

For a comfier den, sweep the floor to make it smooth, then cover it with rugs, old sacks or blankets. If the ground is damp, use a groundsheet or Karrimats to stay dry.

HOW TO MAKE WATERPROOF DENS

Making a den waterproof is a challenge. Cover it with large tarps or plastic sheeting. Pull the cover tight and set it at a steep angle so rain runs off quickly.

Here's a handy tip for collecting lots of leaves to cover a den: pile them up in a big heap on a rug or tarp. It makes it so much easier to transport them to your den.

Believe it or not, you can make a natural den waterproof by using only a few sticks, finished off with a thick thatch of leaves; see for yourself on page 86.

Be inventive and experiment. These children used a gutter to take rain away from the den; it didn't work very well, but they had fun trying to come up with their own design.

DEN FIXINGS

To store string: cut a plastic bottle in half, put string inside, tape the bottle back together, then cut a hole in the lid to thread the string through.

Pegs are a handy way to fix things in place. Tie things together with bungees, rope, string, garden twine or torn-up strips of fabric, such as old sheets.

Bulldog clips and clothes pegs are a quick way to fix things in place, but use cable ties or a hammer and nails for stronger fixings.

If you are making a natural den, use natural fixings such as ivy or wild clematis stems or blackberry runners. Whatever you can find.

THE BOWLINE KNOT

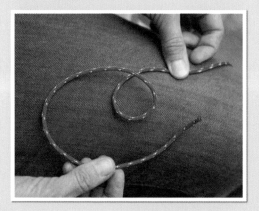

If you only learn one knot, make it the bowline. This secure loop at the end of a rope or string won't tighten or slip under strain, but is quick to tie and untie.

Make a small loop near one end of a rope. Thread the rope end up through the loop and under the main line of the rope as shown.

Now bring the rope end back over the main line of rope and back down through the small loop to form the knot.

Pull the rope end and the main rope simultaneously to tighten and make a neat and secure knot as above.

MAKING TENT PEGS

If you are making a tent-like den (see pages 20 and 32), you will need tent pegs and guy ropes to secure the cover in place. Make tent pegs out of sticks; hazel is ideal but any green wood should be okay. Cut a length of about 25cm/10in and use a sharp knife (see Den Safety on page 140) to whittle one end to a point. Carve a notch at the other end of the stick and then scrape off the bark if you wish.

ATTACHING GUY ROPES

Use rope or string for guy ropes. Attach them to your fabric, by placing a small nut or stone in the corner of the fabric.

Tie string tightly around to secure the stone or nut in place, as illustrated above. Now loop guy rope around the stone so it holds firm.

DECORATIVE DEN DETAILS

Add details to welcome your friends or scare off possible invaders. Old tyres and play tunnels make great entrances, too small for grownups!

Transform a woodland den into a flower-fairy palace by decorating with leaf bunting, flower chains and perhaps magic wands.

Make a garden den into a warrior's hideout with camouflage, stick weapons, warning bells and escape routes.

Make seats from fallen logs, wooden boxes or even an old tyre. Or make a bed in a hammock or a pile of leaves.

Dress a garden-tent den with some brightly coloured cushions, blankets and a few favourite toys for a relaxing chill-out pad.

To store things in or near your den, a net hammock keeps your bags dry and off the ground, or you could use handy twigs as coat hooks.

Make a den play area by fencing off a patch around your den. Hang a rope swing from a sturdy branch and secure with rope.

Make your den more secure with a look-out point, a trap door, an alarm system or a bell to announce visitors.

DEN FEASTS

Dens are perfect places for enjoying tasty snacks, sharing a picnic with friends or cooking a meal over a nearby fire.

Try cooking an outdoor meal over a fire in a fire pan or make your own special cooking fireplace, like this one made from bricks.

How about warm cocoa with marshmallows in your den on a cold, rainy day? Or golden slice followed by baked bananas?

If no real food is available, just make gloopy mud pancakes or fantastic festive mud cakes for a pretend feast instead.

GOLDEN SLICE

Chop and fry one onion and mix with 140g (5oz) oats, 115g (4oz) grated cheddar cheese, 170g (6oz) grated carrot, 1 beaten egg, 55g (2oz) melted butter, 1tbsp dried rosemary and a little salt and pepper. Press the mixture into a greased shallow baking tin. Bake at 180C for about 20 minutes until the top is golden brown. Cut into portions.

BAKED BANANAS

Peel bananas and slit each one lengthways. Put two pieces of chocolate into each banana, or mix together equal quantities of butter and muscovado sugar (molasses) and put a spoonful of the mixture in each banana. Wrap the bananas in foil. Bake over a fire for about 20 minutes. Carefully remove the foil packages from the fire. Cool a little before unwrapping.

DEN SAFETY

We hope you have fun making dens, but please follow these guidelines to help you and wild places stay safe.

LEAVING NO TRACE
- Respect all wildlife and be considerate to other users of wild places.
- Anything you take out with you must go home with you, including all den-making materials and rubbish.
- Take responsibility for your own actions.
- Only collect loose and plant materials that are common and in abundance.

FIRE SAFETY GUIDELINES
Always follow these guidelines when using fire or candles:
- Never make a fire unless you have permission to do so and adults are around to supervise.
- Make a fire on mineral soil, in a pit or (preferably) in a fire pan.
- Never light a fire in windy or excessively dry weather.
- Never leave a fire or a candle unattended.
- Have a supply of water nearby to extinguish the fire or soothe burns.
- Use as little wood as you can and let the fire burn down to ash. Once it is cold, remove all traces of your fire.

TOOL AND WEAPON SAFETY GUIDELINES
- Make sure everyone is aware of the potential dangers of using sharp tools and homemade weapons; accidents often happen when people mess around.
- Only use a knife if you have been given permission and have been shown how to use them safely. Always have a first-aid kit handy, and make sure someone knows how to use it.
- Before using a knife, make sure there is an imaginary no-entry zone all around you. To check, stand up with your arms spread out and turn around;

you shouldn't be able to touch anyone or anything.

- Never cut over your lap – the femoral artery in the thigh carries large volumes of blood and, if severed, you will lose a pint of blood per minute.
- Work the blade away from your body and from the hand supporting the wood. Never cut towards your hand until you can use a knife with great control.
- If you need to pass a knife to someone else, always do so with the handle pointing towards the other person.
- Always put tools away when not in use; never leave them lying around.
- Treat knives and other sharp tools with respect: always stick to the rules.

It is safest to make a fire in mineral soil, in a pit or in a firepan. Keep a supply of water nearby to extinguish flames if needs be.

When using a knife, always cut away from you and never over your lap. Always pass a knife to someone else by the handle only.

INDEX

THANKS AND ACKNOWLEDGMENTS

MANY THANKS TO:

The families and friends who have built dens with us, and to everyone who made wonderful dens for us to discover!

All the young people who took part in den activities: Elsa, Freddie and Maggie G; Anya, Clifford and Frankie C; Daisy and Monty S; Libby and George W; Calum and Rhona M; Matthew and Romily M; Adam and Natasha H; James and Maria M; Gabriel and Ri Gavin; Tiggy W; Charlie, Lily and Toby R; Tom U; Jo B; Tristan S; Jonathan A; Jack D; Nicholas V; Ayrton and Edward K; Edward and Rebecca W; Tilly S; Jonny F; Sophie T; Matt and Tris E; Alex B; Amelia, Digby and George B; Betty and Marcus B; Laura V; George W; Romily M; Yanni K; Amy, Annabel and Matilda S; Joel R; Alberto, Edu and Robi SM; Cal, Katie and Tom SJ; Kate W; Ella W; Lucas R; Megan S; and the children in Polly Scott's reception class and at the Treehouse School.

THE FOLLOWING PEOPLE AND ORGANISATIONS FOR THEIR HELP:

Jane and Bob White; Judith and George Oakes; Anita Osborne (willow weaver).
White City Adventure Playground www.facebook.com/WhiteCityPlay
The Treehouse School www.thetreehouseschool.org.uk
Marieke McBean www.marieke.co.uk
Stuart Turner, creator of Hazel, the dragon of Magdalen Wood
stuartlandart@googlemail.com
Streatley Wildwood, location of the Wild Outdoor Feast,
www.streatleywildwood.co.uk
Cogges Manor Farm www.cogges.org.uk

Our husbands, Ben and Peter and our children, Jake, Dan, Connie, Hannah and Edward.

And finally, thanks to everyone at Frances Lincoln.